Mouthing Off

EXPLOITS OF AN OUTSPOKEN ANCHORWOMAN

ANNETTE ESTES

Mouthing Off
Annette Estes

Copyright © 2019 Annette Estes

Published by 1st World Publishing
P.O. Box 2211, Fairfield, Iowa 52556
tel: 641-209-5000 • fax: 866-440-5234
web: www.1stworldpublishing.com

First Edition
Library of Congress Cataloging-in-Publication Data
Softcover ISBN: 978-0-9744894-1-4

All rights reserved. Printed in the United States of America. No part of this book may be used or reproduced in any manner whatsoever without written permission except in the case of brief quotations embodied in critical articles and reviews.

Dedication

Dedicated to my former colleagues and viewers – and to Scott, his buddies, and the woman in the café who years later asked me, "Did you really say that on TV?"

Appreciations

First and foremost, I thank the viewers who liked me and watched our nightly newscasts. Thanks for the letters and continued support today on Facebook.

Thanks to management and colleagues of the two TV stations where we worked together. I still love all of you. And I don't hate any of you.

Thanks also to Jay Mattsson for his superb editing and Rodney Charles for publishing extraordinaire.

About the Author

Annette Estes has had three careers: from teaching to television to training. She began her professional career teaching high school English and speech in Louisville, Kentucky, and Jeffersonville, Indiana, before getting her first on-air television job in Louisville.

After a 15-year career as a news anchor she began her own business and is now a Certified Professional Behavioral and Values Analyst, Coach, and Managing Director of The Estes Group, an employee job-performance management company, specializing in helping companies hire, develop, and retain the right people.

Annette is an alumna of the University of the Ozarks. She was named "Outstanding Senior Woman" in 1967 and in 1980 was chosen by her college as "The Student of the Decade." She's also a graduate of Coach U, and a founding member of CoachVille and the International Association of Coaches. She is an award-winning author, columnist, and professional speaker.

Annette lives in Fairfield, IA.

For more information on The Estes Group, visit http://www.coachannette.com

Table of Contents

Preface xi
Chapter 1 - A Desire that Lingered 1
Chapter 2 - A Dream that Lingered 8
Chapter 3 - Facing Inequality 12
Chapter 4 - The Team that Plays Together 23
Chapter 5 - Good News, Bad News 30
Chapter 6 - Seeing Stars 38
Chapter 7 - Rumors, Rumors 46
Chapter 8 - Bloops and Bleeps 49
Chapter 9 - It's Too Hot to F***? 52
Chapter 10 - The Fallout 57
Chapter 11 - Moving On 64
Chapter 12 - Changing Channels 67
Chapter 13 - Life After Broadcasting 77
Chapter 14 - Film at 11:00 82
Photo Gallery 89

Preface

"...everyone will be world-famous for 15 minutes."
                                              Andy Warhol

Some people will have 15 seconds, minutes, or days of fame. I had 15 years.

Well, not world fame, but I was a TV news anchor from 1977 to 1992 in one of America's top forty television markets – ten years at the CBS affiliate WSPA, Channel 7 and five years at the NBC affiliate WYFF, Channel 4. Or maybe it was "infamy." We'll see.

I'm not going to identify most of the people I worked with during that time by their actual names – to protect the guilty.

To keep similar stories together, I sometimes skip around from year-to-year, station-to-station, anchor-to-anchor. I hope this doesn't confuse you.

The idea for writing this book came on a hot July day in 2008. The temperatures had been 100+ degrees for several days.

That afternoon I got a phone call at my home/office from a man named Scott. He said he'd been a big fan of mine when I was a news anchor and that whenever it was extremely hot, he and his buddies would think of me. Someone would say,

"Boy, it's HOT!" Another would ask, "How hot is it?" In unison they would all answer, "It's too hot to F***!"

I knew he was misquoting what I had actually said on-air (unawares) on that hot July day in 1986. I told him the true story and said he should tell his buddies what I really said. He said, "No way," that this was a long-standing ritual they had and telling them the truth would spoil all their fun.

I said okay. If I can be a catalyst for making people laugh and have fun, even at my own expense, then that's all right with me.

So, a year later, in July of 2009, I began writing this book. (I got sidelined for a while taking care of my mother and moving to another state after she died, then taking care of my brother.)

I hope you enjoy the stories – positive and negative – humorous and serious – famous and infamous.

They are all true.

And I will reveal what I actually said during that newscast in July, 1986.

Sorry, Scott and buddies.

1

A Desire that Lingered

Someone once wrote that when you have a desire that won't go away, it's the voice of God telling you that you should have it. That's how my television news career began.

It took hold when I read Barbara Walter's book, *How to Talk to Practically Anybody about Practically Anything*. I wanted to do what she did – interview people on television – although I didn't want to be as "tough" on people as she was. I wanted to be one of those female co-hosts of a local morning talk show.

I got my first on-air job when I was teaching high school speech and English in Jeffersonville, Indiana. One day the general managers of the three local television stations in Louisville, Kentucky, came to the school to encourage teachers to use instructional TV programs in our classes.

During the question and answer session, I asked, "How does one get an on-air job in television?" The GMs said come to the station and audition.

So, I did.

Miss Annette

A few months later, I came home one day and my husband, Bob, told me the ABC affiliate station – WLKY-TV – had called me. We wondered if they were going to offer me a job, and if so what? We checked the local TV listings and he said, "I'll bet it's *Romper Room*." I said, "No way."

He was right. My first job as a TV on-air personality was as Miss Annette of *Romper Room*. The station sent me to Baltimore to learn how to host the show from Bert and Nancy Claster, creators of the popular children's program.

I spent two hours each weekday morning (making $100 a week) taping the show. I asked the principal of my school if I could have my two free periods in the morning and come in late so I could do both jobs. But he said no. So, I gave up my high school teaching career to teach preschoolers. But it was on TV!

Like Art Linkletter, I could write a book on the darndest things children say. But I'll just relate a couple of them.

Even though *Romper Room* was taped, it might as well have been live, because the director wouldn't stop the tape except in the case of a dire emergency, which fortunately we never had. Once after a show we did have to capture a ferret that had gotten loose and scampered up into the studio lights.

We interrupt this story to say: Our director was given the task of figuring out how to keep the teacher on the show if she got pregnant. He suggested taping six months in advance (and something about airing some of them backwards?)

But I didn't get pregnant, so we didn't have to worry about offending the viewers. Do you suppose they didn't know where all of our guest children came from???

It was 1969; we were still in the dark ages of sex discrimination.

Anyway, back to our scheduled programming. I often did "live" commercials during *Romper Room*. One day as I was extolling the virtues of Colgate toothpaste, one little boy piped up at the top of his lungs, "Miss Annette, I use something better than that. I use Crest!"

Needless to say, we gave Colgate a "make good" spot at no charge.

Another time, the six children and I were discussing their favorite games. Most of them were tag, hide-and-seek, and the like. One of the twin brothers on the show that week told us that, "Our favorite game is Candyland. But the kitty pooped on it and we had to throw it out!"

I thought we were going to have to give the mothers sitting in the studio CPR they were laughing so hard. How I kept a relatively straight face, I'll never know. My acting training, I guess. (I'd majored in speech and drama in college.)

Romper, Bomper, Stomper, Boo!

Moving Ahead

After a brief stint in a behind-the-scenes job at WHAS-TV, I came back to WLKY at the behest of their new GM as the Community Affairs Coordinator. They had let the Community Affairs Director go and hired me to replace him with a lesser title and probably half the pay. My first – but not last – encounter with corporate salary discrimination. But I was young and happy to be there.

Soon, the station created a five-minute talk show for me that aired weekday mornings. We called it *Rap it Up!* That was back when "rap" just meant "talk."

I mostly interviewed local folks about a program or event of community interest. But I also sometimes got to interview celebrities.

In addition, I was given reporting jobs and a five-minute news and weathercast in the mornings. I was on my way!

WLKY had one female reporter. Her name was Diane Sawyer. I knew back then that she would be a network correspondent someday.

You already know she is beautiful and intelligent; I can tell you she is also one of the nicest people I've ever met.

There is one thing I don't appreciate about Diane, though. She still looks the same age she was when I worked with her!

Speaking of popular network correspondents, one visited our affiliate station and I got to interview him during my newscast. He was handsome, smart, and charming. After he left, as I was filing my script, I noticed he had written on one page:

You made a mistake on this one, Annette
Peter Jennings

To this day, I wonder what the mistake was, or if he was just teasing me. I also wonder whatever happened to the original of that script I copied. His death was a great and untimely loss.

Who knew on that day that I was in the same building with two future ABC Nightly News anchors?

Great Scott!

If you were to ask me the best thing that happened to me at WLKY-TV, I'd have to say it was my interview with one of Hollywood's greatest actors. And equally rewarding – the way I got the interview.

Louisville hosted a gala event to celebrate the opening of the Gen. George S. Patton, Jr. museum in Fort Knox. The guest of honor – actor George C. Scott who starred in the film *Patton*, which won seven academy award Oscars, including best actor.

The other two local stations both had hour-long morning talk shows with male and female co-hosts – the kind of job I wanted, remember. They had pooled their resources and built a lovely set they would share to interview him.

I wasn't invited.

Our news director, John Sharp, and I were waiting in the room filled with onlookers, when Mr. Scott came in. John immediately introduced us and asked if I could interview him (standing in a corner of the room with a cinderblock background). He said yes. Way to go, John!

Moments later, the hosts of the talk show who had won the coin toss with the other station to interview him first, came up to him and proceeded to lead him to their "set."

He said to them, "Surely, but I promised this young lady the first interview."

The man endeared himself to me for life. When our interview began, I called him "General Patton," then corrected myself. He beamed and said, "Thank you."

I don't remember what we said during that interview. I only remember being thankful that although my knees were literally knocking together, my hand holding the microphone was steady. Also, it was pretty cool not to have to share the interview with a co-host.

And even cooler to have the other stations' hosts watching and waiting their turn. ☺

From that moment on, George C. Scott could do no wrong.

Whoa, Pardner!

I had the pleasure of interviewing Roy Rogers and Dale Evans when their rodeo show came to town. Well, Dale anyway. They were waiting in a basement room at the arena when I arrived. Dale was friendly and we got a great interview with her.

But during the whole time, Roy paced back and forth along a wall of lockers and was still going when we left.

Goodbye, Mr. Popcorn

Eventually, I left the station, not of my own volition. My guest on *Rap it Up* one morning was to be Orville Redenbacher. But the afternoon before, the new general manager called me into his office and told me I was outta there.

I wondered who would interview the popcorn mogul. I watched the next morning and wasn't surprised to see the hot, young blonde "babe" who'd been working as a secretary do the interview. (I was still a brunette then.)

I didn't watch again and it was a long time before I could eat Orville Redenbacher's popcorn. But I got over it and now eat it with relish! No, actually with ghee.

Recipe for Disaster

Speaking of food magnates, there was one scary yet rather amusing incident that occurred around that time. One Sunday morning my husband and I were driving on I-65 on our way to church, when a car entered the highway to our right. The driver failed to slow down and would have hit us if Bob hadn't quickly pulled into the left lane.

As we passed the car, I looked over at the driver and there – dressed in all his white regalia – was KFC's Col. Harlan Sanders.

Never interviewed him, but still love his original recipe.

One note about *Romper Room*. It was a franchised local program, not a nationally broadcast show like *Capt. Kangaroo*. All of the teachers and children on the show were from the town where they lived. They were your friends and neighbors.

When I would tell someone I'd done *Romper Room*, they'd ask, "Oh, were you Miss Pat, or Ruth, or Betsy?"

"No, I was Miss Annette."

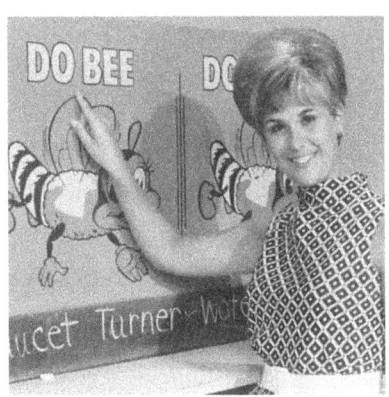

2

A Dream that Lingered

When my husband finished his oral surgery residency in 1972, we moved back to his home state. I put my television dream job on hold to be a housewife and later to work for him when he began his solo practice.

But the TV bug kept biting. One night in 1977, I had a dream that I went back to college to get a master's degree in journalism so I could get hired as a TV news anchor. The dream stayed with me and I decided to act on it. I applied to two universities and talked with Bob about it.

Good Advice

I made a trip back to Louisville to talk with the news director at WLKY, Rick Moore. He and I had worked together – even shared an office – before I left. I told him of my plans and asked for his advice.

He said, "Annette, news directors don't want people with master's degrees. They want people with experience." (Sounds like Charlie the Tuna.) He told me I needed a demo tape. He was kind enough to give me some old news scripts and made the demo tape for me as I "anchored" from their news set.

I came home and showed the tape to the WSPA and WYFF news directors. They didn't hire me. But WSPA did create a children's program I hosted for a while. I named it *Confabulation*.

Eventually, I told the general manager at WSPA that I'd be willing to work for free in the news department to get experience for a paying job.

He agreed and I began working as a non-paid behind-the-scenes reporter in 1977. I wrote stories, shot and edited film for the newscasts.

I moved into an apartment, as my husband and I decided to get divorced. It was amicable and we still talk on the phone from time to time, even though we never had children.

After three months of working as an unpaid intern, I told the WSPA general manager that I couldn't afford to do that anymore and they needed to hire and pay me or I was going to have to look for a job elsewhere.

WSPA hired me as their weekend news anchor. Yes!

Oh, neither university accepted my application, which is just as well since I would have turned them down anyway.

I was getting real-life, real-job experience. And a salary!

The Anchor Desk

After a few months, WSPA decided to make me the co-anchor of the 6:00 and 11:00 weeknight newscasts. The other two stations in the market both had male and female co-anchors. I was the first woman to anchor the primary newscasts at WSPA. (And it was a whole lot better than doing a morning talk show.)

When my co-anchor, Dan, left for a bigger market, I anchored alone for a few months until WSPA found his replacement, Scott.

Scott was one of my favorite co-anchors of the five I shared the news desk with over my 15-year career.

OOPS!

During the time of my solo anchoring, I came to work one day and found some papers on my desk that weren't mine. The only other people in the newsroom at the time were a reporter and our weekend sports anchor, Jack. (He was also one of my favorite colleagues.)

I realized the papers were the salary list of the entire news department. I told the others and Jack grabbed them and made copies. We put the original on the news director's desk.

After studying the list, I saw that a reporter – an older man who worked as a bureau chief in another town – was being paid considerably more than I was. I thought that was unfair and told the general manager so. He said they were grooming this man to be an anchor. I told him that until then they should increase my salary, to be fair.

They did.

I gained some admirers and detractors for doing that, but I knew if I didn't stand up for myself, no one else would. Thus, began my career as an outspoken anchorwoman. That's how I describe it. I'm sure others had a more unflattering term.

An Unhappy Viewer

One night during the time of my solo-anchoring as I was producing the 11:00 newscast, the switchboard operator rang the newsroom and asked me if I'd talk to this "crazy" woman on the phone.

I said okay and answered, "Newsroom." The caller didn't know she was talking to me.

She launched into a tirade about how terrible it was that Annette Estes had taken Dan's job. I told her Annette didn't take his job, that she was doing her own job and that he'd left to get a higher-paying one.

The woman continued by saying a woman shouldn't be doing a man's job, that she should be home with her husband and if she didn't have a husband, she should be out working to get one. (*Oh, please.*)

I finally said, "Ma'am, we think Annette's doing a good job and we're going to keep her. Thanks for calling. Goodbye."

I wonder if it was the same woman who called me at home fifteen years later to say some very unpleasant things. More on that later.

Walt Kelly was right. "We have met the enemy and (s)he is us."

3

Facing Inequality

The first blatant encounter with gender bias that I recall happened to me at WHAS-TV in Louisville back in 1970. When WLKY cancelled *Romper Room*, I was hired by the station's former general manager – who had moved to WHAS – to work in the traffic department helping put the daily broadcast log together.

When I learned that WHAS was looking for a new on-air weather forecaster (i.e. weatherman), I told the GM I'd like to have the job. (This was years before TV stations began hiring meteorologists.)

He said, "Oh, no; we can't hire a woman to do the weather. It would be too gimmicky."

End of conversation.

I honestly don't believe he had any idea how sexist and insulting his statement was. That's just the way women were thought of back then.

It's interesting to note, however, that WSPA-TV had an on-air "weather girl" (geez) for years before hiring me to anchor the news.

Show Me the Money

As far as salary goes, probably the highest-paying job I'd had up to this point was *Romper Room*. I was making $10 an hour as Miss Annette. Not too shabby for 1970.

After getting the raise at WSPA to bring my salary more in line with a news anchor position, I don't believe I ever faced salary discrimination again during my TV news career. Indeed, I eventually became the highest-paid anchor in the market.

But I did continue to experience other types of inequality, as did many of my female colleagues.

As we saw in the last chapter, some women buy into discrimination against their gender, believing the societal myth that women are second-class citizens.

Those of us who refused to accept that treatment back in the '70s faced a tough battle and usually earned the title "prima donna," "diva," or "bitch," which in themselves are words used to discredit and criticize assertive women. Although some emotionally secure women consider those labels to be a compliment, even if they are meant to be derogatory. After all, Bitch stands for "Being in total control of herself."

In my case, I believe my high salary, while being great for me personally, was the source of resentment among some – but certainly not all – of my colleagues. Some men have problems working with women who make more money than they do.

Sex Discrimination's Many Forms

One of the first things to happen that made me uncomfortable was WSPA's idea to do a promo with the anchor team frolicking in a swimming pool. I was told to wear a bikini. I hated doing that, but had no choice. Today I'd refuse; but then today no one would ask me to pose in a bikini. ☺

But you get my point. How did my prancing around in a skimpy swimsuit with three men increase my credibility as a newswoman?

It didn't.

I don't know how the men felt about it.

No, thanks, I've got a headache

Then there was the time I was hit on by fellow reporter, Peter. He was a nice married guy whom everyone liked, but he sort of jokingly propositioned me one night as I was editing film in the newsroom.

I didn't want to make a scene, so I turned him down by saying I wasn't attracted to him.

It worked. He walked away, we remained friends, and he never bothered me again. Well, I take that back. Years later the station sent us to Los Angeles on assignment for several days. One night after a group of us came back to the hotel from having dinner, I'd been in my room less than five minutes when my phone rang.

Peter said in a humorous way, "I know it's late, but I'll come up and give you a quickie if you want me to." I laughed and said something like, "No thanks, I have a headache." And that was it.

I learned with some men, using humor or insulting their egos can work like a charm. My advice to women is to try that first. But if a man at work aggressively pursues or sexually harasses you, report it to management and insist that it cease. If not, then talk to your attorney.

I know some office relationships are mutual, but it's been my observation that it's just not a good idea to get involved with someone at work, especially a boss, subordinate, or married co-worker.

Higher Degrees of Sexual Harassment

One on-air incident occurred at the expense of our noon anchor, Joan. The WSPA noon weatherman reported one day the local temperature was 69 degrees. He looked into the camera and said, "69 – that's Joan's favorite temperature."

I didn't see the newscast, but my co-anchor Brad told me about it as soon as I got to work. Like everyone else, I was horrified and asked him if Joan had complained to management about such a blatant, public slur on her character. He said he didn't think so. He and I talked with Joan and encouraged her to stand up for herself and not let that kind of sexist behavior be tolerated. She talked with the general manager.

I'm not sure exactly what happened, but apparently the weather guy denied saying that. He was dating a young woman who worked in engineering. The general manager and news director looked at the show tape and discovered that his comment had been erased. Our own little "weathergate." He and his girlfriend were both fired.

My advice: Always take personal responsibility for your actions. Own up to your mistakes and make amends in whatever way is necessary and appropriate. Covering up will always get you in more trouble than if you admit to and apologize for your mistakes or poor judgment and behavior.

Subtle, but Deadly

Sometimes sexual harassment is much more subtle (thank goodness) but still hurtful. Every incident can chip away at one's self-esteem and even a strong woman can get discouraged over time.

Once I was doing a series on rape and was looking at the segment I'd done for that night's newscast in the tape room. One engineer turned to me and said didn't I know that rape was impossible?

Huh?

"Yeah," he said. "Everyone knows a woman can run faster with her dress pulled up than a man with his pants down."

Perhaps I should have said nothing, but the emotion of interviewing rape victims was still with me; so, I told him what I thought of his little "joke" and walked out.

The Dildo

This story happened later at WYFF, but I'll skip ahead and include it here.

One afternoon when I got to work, I opened my desk drawer and there was a life-sized, very realistic rubber penis inside. As was my nature back then, I got upset and accused our noon anchor, Kevin, who was an accomplished practical joker. He swore he didn't do it, but I'm sure everyone enjoyed my being the butt of a newsroom joke.

Later one of our reporters, Jim, confessed to being the one who'd placed it there. I couldn't be too upset at that point and besides, he was one of my favorite people at WYFF.

Skip ahead to 2008. Jim, the reporter, is now working in another field and has written a play. The play is being performed at a local theater with a friend of mine, Donna, directing it.

It was a hit and on closing night I gave Donna and Jim each a gift bag. When Jim reached into his bag, he immediately jerked his hand out and said no way was he taking that out of the bag. So, I did it for him. I wish I could say it was the same rubber penis he'd given me, but I'd given it to Kevin, who's gay.

We had a good laugh showing it to the cast and telling the story. Revenge is sweet!

Not So Funny

There were other sexual harassment incidents at WYFF, which were really out of line.

The man who directed the newscasts would come into the newsroom each afternoon to put the scripts together and would loudly regale us with a litany of dirty jokes. No one ever stopped him. He may still be there doing that for all I know.

Surely not.

This one I still can't believe. When I first began anchoring at WYFF, I noticed something happening that appalled me. I pretended I didn't notice and asked my co-anchor, Kent, how did our weatherman, Chuck, know whether to throw it back to him or me at the end of the weathercast?

He laughed and said if Chuck was supposed to throw it back to me, the floor person (often a young woman) would point to her breasts. If he was to throw it back to Kent, she pointed to her crotch.

Excuse me, but does anyone besides me find it grossly

inappropriate for a young woman to have to point to her boobs or her crotch to cue the weatherman???

I told the newly-hired news director, who was unaware of this apparently long-standing, on-going method of studio communication. He put an immediate stop to it by having cue cards with the anchors' (from every newscast) names printed on them. The floor person held them under the camera lens to cue Chuck. What a novel idea.

I suppose I became immediately unpopular for spoiling all their fun, but surely someone besides the news director agreed with me. If so, they never said anything.

Professional Biases

Other types of discrimination (gender, racial, etc.) are more professionally-oriented. Gee, that almost sounds nice by comparison.

One way men subtly discriminate against women is to ignore them. Once, WSPA co-anchor Rob and I were interviewing a U.S. senator during a taped half-hour public affairs show. I was wearing a pantsuit and the senator obviously disapproved. During the entire program he talked only to Rob, even when I had asked him a question.

One of my colleagues who obviously didn't like me much was Sam, the sports anchor at WSPA. At one point for quite a while, he did the same thing as the senator. He never looked at me – only at Scott – during the transitions in and out of the sportscast. I just considered the source and tolerated it.

Once we were all in a meeting with the general manager, Vernon, and Sam was complaining about something.

I remember Vernon changing the subject by asking Sam why he never looked at me during the newscast.

I said, "You've actually noticed that?" He said, "Yes," and told Sam to knock it off and start acting like the team member he was supposed to be.

I imagine Sam thought I'd complained to Vernon, but I hadn't. That was one of the few times anyone stood up for me without my asking them to. It felt good.

Once a newly-hired news director at WSPA was talking with Rob and me and made a comment about "the anchor and the co-anchor." Rob and I looked at each other, both knowing he meant Rob was the anchor and I was the "co-anchor." Rob said I should go "straighten him out."

So, I politely told the news director that Rob and I considered ourselves to be equals, that we were both co-anchors. But if there was to be an anchor and a co-anchor, then I was the anchor because I'd been working at WSPA longer. He didn't call us that again.

That reminds me of something I accomplished at WSPA that I've never told anyone and don't know if anyone I worked with knew my real motivation.

I had noticed that local news stations around the country that had hired female co-anchors to join men who'd been anchoring solo always placed the man to the right of the woman. On every newscast that I saw, the man was always on the left of the screen during a camera two-shot.

Whether that was intended, or the suggestion of a news consultant, or whatever, the male anchor always occupied that position. And society being what it was, it became the dominant anchor spot.

When I began co-anchoring with Dan at WSPA, he sat to

my right. When he left, I anchored from the center and when Scott was hired, I asked the general manager if I could have the seat to his right as I had seniority. He said okay.

I don't know, but I think from 1977-87 I may have been the only woman anchor in the United States occupying the screen-left anchor seat. If other women anchors also did during that time, please let me hear from you.

I noticed when I left WSPA in 1987, my replacement took my seat; but it wasn't long before they traded anchor seats – back to the old way – and put her on Brad's left. Well, he did have seniority.

When I went to WYFF, I sat to the left of my co-anchor for the first time since I'd shared the anchor desk with Dan. It felt strange, but I didn't mind because he had seniority there. Fair's fair.

I did enjoy my ten years being in what the industry considered the main anchor's seat, though; and I guess no one else minded. All of my co-anchors and I considered ourselves equals and that's what really mattered.

Evolving Language

It was during the 1980s that our language became more noticeably "politically correct." I remember during a taped news story once, the reporter referred to the "chairperson."

I turned to Rob and said, "Have you noticed that these days men are men and women are persons?"

He grimaced and agreed. It was a long time before people felt comfortable even saying the word "woman."

But even back then the word "chairwoman" sounded all right to me.

I remember back during my news days at WLKY-TV, one of our more enlightened technical directors introduced me as "newswoman, Annette Estes."

You'd have thought he'd suggested we all do the news naked from management's horrified reaction. So, they continued introducing me as, "Here with the story is newsman, Annette Estes."

Sounds silly now, doesn't it?

Ageism

The same news director at WSPA who made the anchor/co-anchor remark told me one day that local TV news was unfair to women. He said men can anchor till their hair turns grey but when female anchors turn thirty, they're replaced by a younger woman. I said I guess I was pretty lucky, then, since I was thirty-five.

I lasted as a television news anchor until I was one month from turning 48, which was a milestone in the early '90s. Now I'm pleased to see my former colleagues and other aging female anchors hanging in there with the men. Although, in some markets that trend still seems the norm – older man, younger woman.

Heck, one of my former stations hired a female meteorologist (not a "gimmick") who looked around the age I am now.

Maybe I'll go apply for another anchor job!

Maybe not.

TAG: For the record, while I still don't like discrimination of any kind, I don't hate it either. To hate anything, any situation, or any person only destroys one's peace of mind and doesn't change anything. Change comes from within as human consciousness grows and evolves.

I take these words from Jesus Christ to heart:

> "...*Verily I say unto you, Inasmuch as ye have done* it *unto one of the least of these my brethren, ye have done* it *unto me.*"
> — Matthew 25:40
> *King James Bible*

4

The Team that Plays Together

By far, the majority of my relationships with my colleagues, co-workers, and managers were positive and fun. I got along swimmingly ☺ with all of my co-anchors at WSPA – Dan, Scott, Rob, Brad, and later Kent (at WYFF). Brad was the only seriously introverted one, earning him the nickname, "the man from Neptune" from the sports guys.

Rob was somewhat introverted, but very funny. One time he called a local political office winner the day after an election, pretending to be the famous senator from the man's party. (The same senator who didn't like pantsuits on women.)

Rob imitated the senator's voice so perfectly he convinced the new state representative he was calling personally from Washington to congratulate him. I don't know if anyone ever told the man it wasn't really the senator; so, if he's reading this – sorry about that.

The co-anchor I enjoyed most at WSPA-TV was Scott. He and I had similar behavioral styles and good on-air chemistry.

Thanksgiving Traditions

Our sports anchor Sam (he was talking to me again) and his wife gave many of us something to be grateful for every Thanksgiving. They invited station "orphans" to their home for Thanksgiving dinner. Those of us who had to work and didn't have family in the area got to feast together and enjoy the holiday with our TV "family." That was nice of them.

The next day the anchor team always rode the WSPA-TV float in the annual Christmas Parade. Oh, joy.

Once to "take the chill off," Scott made up a large batch of mimosas. We started drinking them before the parade started.

This was during the Iranian hostage crisis right after American women and African Americans had been released by their captors. Our weekend anchor Greg, a charming, handsome black man, and I decided to hit the port-a-potties before we took off. He and I walked down the street proclaiming loudly, "Women and blacks first! Women and blacks first!"

Very mature of us.

When the parade finally ended, Scott and our meteorologist, Kyle, jumped off the float and ran down an embankment next to the railroad tracks to relieve themselves of their mimosas. Greg and I were fine.

Meeting Our Mentors

Every now and then our CBS network would invite its affiliate anchor teams to come to New York City to do interviews and promos with the network news anchors and correspondents. Once Scott and I went to work with legendary CBS anchor Walter Cronkite. Scott had arrived before I did.

When I got to the hotel and checked into my room, I noticed men's clothes and toiletries strewn about. The hotel had obviously put me in the wrong room and as I went to call the front desk, I saw a note from Scott which began, "Hi, Roomie!"

I told the hotel clerk I needed my own room, but he said there were no other rooms available. I asked him to put me in another hotel, but he said he couldn't do that.

So, Scott and I were stuck sharing a room. We were good friends, but not *that* close. Still, we made the most of it. At least there were two beds so he didn't have to sleep on the floor.

But it all worked out okay; and working with Walter Cronkite was a local news anchor's dream assignment.

Politics, Poise, and Persistence

Scott and I shared the duty of covering the national political conventions. Speaking of Walter Cronkite, I got to witness a funny incident at the Dallas GOP Convention in 1984.

We all had to walk through metal detectors to get into the convention hall. I was walking in the corridor and saw Mr. Cronkite come in one evening and cause the detector's alarm to sound. A security guard frisked him thoroughly and I got to see a side of "Uncle Walter" most people never saw.

He looked, as they say, as mad as an old wet hen.

I covered the Carter-Mondale Democratic National Convention in New York City in 1980. Afternoons were slow, so I decided to visit my native state's delegation – Arkansas – which was up front near the podium.

I stopped near the Vermont delegation, next to Arkansas.

One delegate had his baby daughter in a back sling. I held my finger up and she grabbed it. Then I heard a whir of cameras snapping and looked up to see a horde of photographers taking our picture. Their cameras had really big lenses.

My news reporter's credo of accuracy kicked in so I yelled up to them that I was a reporter, not a delegate. But, sure enough, the next morning in *The New York Times*, there was our picture. The caption identified Jim Leddy and his daughter Giovanna, then said the infant "played with a friendly *delegate* as she sat comfortably in a carrier on her father's back." Proof you can't believe everything you read in the newspapers.

I just Googled and found out Jim Leddy went on to become a Vermont state senator. Giovanna is a bariatric physician in Boston.

I sent her a copy of this story and the *Times* clipping. She and her parents emailed me back. I've included their emails at the end of the book in the photo section.

That same year, during Ronald Reagan's presidential campaign, his vice-presidential running-mate George H. W. Bush came to our city to speak at a local college.

Scott covered his arrival at the airport and I interviewed him in a campus courtyard. Mr. Bush offhandedly commented that he wished he were still running for president. Eight years later he moved into the White House.

When Scott left WSPA-TV for a bigger market, I was sorry to see him go. Apparently, the station's management was even sorrier because the general manager called me to his office and gave me a $10,000 raise on the spot.

Naturally, I expected that amount with every new contract, but that wasn't gonna happen.

I did see Scott again in 1988 when we covered the Democratic National Convention in Atlanta for our stations. That was the year Gov. Bill Clinton irritated the delegates with his long-winded introduction of presidential nominee, Gov. Michael Dukakis.

One of my state's delegates turned to me and said, "Well, he just blew *his* chance of ever being president!" Right.

The next afternoon as I walked the corridor of the Omni, I saw Gov. Clinton standing alone, everyone passing him by. I sort of felt sorry for him and went over to talk with him and ask him for an autograph for my mother back home in Arkansas. He graciously took her name and address and wrote her a very nice letter.

President Ronald Reagan visited our area on February 6, 1980. I covered his appearance at a local restaurant.

It was his 69th birthday and the owner presented him with a large cake. When President Reagan blew out the candles, he got icing on his tie and laughed. First Lady Nancy wiped it off for him but didn't get the spot out. So, the president took his tie off, gave it to someone to clean, and spoke without it.

Changing Faces

Scott's successor was Rob, a genuinely nice person and accomplished anchorman. He and I were privileged to go to New York (and get separate rooms) when Dan Rather inherited Walter Cronkite's anchor seat. We also taped interviews with other CBS newscasters, including my interview with *60 Minutes* icon Mike Wallace.

Someone once said the four most dreaded words in the English language were, "Mike Wallace is here." I'll admit the ambience in the studio got a little tense when he came in to do the interview.

He and I were sitting on lacquered backless stools waiting for the crew to begin rolling the tape. I was wearing a wool skirt with a nylon slip underneath. As I was making small talk with Mr. Wallace, I felt myself slowly sliding off the seat. At least I managed to land on my feet and not my butt.

We all laughed and the tension was broken.

Go, Hogs!

Back on the anchor desk, Sam used to tease me unmercifully on-air about the Arkansas Razorback hog hat. He made fun of the way it looked and the fans who wore it.

Once while visiting my mother in Arkansas, I bought a hog hat for Sam. I surprised him with it one night going into his sportscast. To be a good sport he had to put it on, but continued to make fun of it. He did look pretty silly, I'll admit.

A Tragic Night

One of the saddest things that happened at WSPA was the tragic loss of two good people in 1990 after I'd left the station. Former weekend sports anchor Jack (of the pilfered salary sheet caper) had been promoted to Sports Director. He and a former WSPA engineer, who was a pilot, were on their way back to the station from a football game when their plane crashed, killing both of them instantly. Jack was one of the best-natured, funniest, and most creative people I've ever known.

Brad was Rob's replacement as my final co-anchor before I left WSPA. He got to share my most famous, infamous, ignoble moment on air. But that deserves a chapter of its own.

Later.

The Team that Plays Together

The Eyewitness News Team, 1986

5

Good News, Bad News

There are people who don't think much of TV news anchors, referring to them derisively as "news readers." This implies all they do is arrive at the studio, have someone do their hair and makeup, and hand them a script on their way to the anchor desk. What a waste of talent and money that would be were it true.

News anchors write many of their own stories daily; they do reporting and occasionally a "series" on a particular subject; and they cover important stories live during newscasts.

I can't say I enjoyed every story I covered, but many stand out as important or enjoyable. I'll mention a few of them here.

Too Much Booze?

The first story I did during my internship at WSPA was a piece on changes in our state's "blue laws," showing what one could and couldn't buy on Sundays.

Our weekend sports anchor, Jack, helped me produce the story. He recorded his voice singing "yes, yes, no, no" to a classical tune as I showed pictures of products. (I told you he was creative.) The story was great except for the fact I edited one strip of film the wrong way. So, viewers saw they couldn't buy their favorite liquor upside down on the shelves.

The Bad News

One weekend as I was about to go home after the 11:00 news, we heard the police scanner talking about a bad car accident. A veteran photographer and I went to the scene.

A group of teenagers was in a car that had hit a gas main, which exploded and set their car on fire. When we arrived, firemen were taking what was left of their charred remains out of the car. The photographer told me, "You don't want to see this." I said, "You're right," and turned my back.

If reporters ever get complacent about seeing such tragedy, they need to get out of the business. Total objectivity is not always a good thing, methinks. Even Walter Cronkite shed tears when the space shuttle Challenger exploded in 1986.

One afternoon at WYFF we got a call that a pit bull had attacked a child. The reporter who took the call was salivating to rush out and cover it. He called to verify the facts and it turned out to be nothing more than something like a toy poodle licked a kid in the face. I may have been the only one in the newsroom who wasn't disappointed.

Once I was asked by a local college to speak to journalism majors. But I would have missed the 6:00 newscast, a big station no-no during sweeps (ratings periods). So, WYFF news director, Allen, took my place.

After the newscast some of us gathered in his office as he told us about his appearance. He said one student asked if it bothered him to be focused so much on negative events every day. I thought, "*Yes, it does.*" But he looked around the room and said, "How could I tell her it's what we thrive on?"

In that respect, I didn't fit in with being a TV news broadcaster.

People tend to believe all the news presented by the media is negative. Not true, but Norman Vincent Peale once pointed out that the news is generally bad because life is intrinsically good; so, when something bad happens, it's news.

And isn't it good it's not the other way around? Imagine if the lead story on your local newscast tonight were, "There were no plane crashes at the airport today." Looking at it that way helped me to survive in an admittedly negative atmosphere.

The Good News

Many of the stories I covered and series I produced for both stations were positive stories of survival. At WSPA I did a series on a man who needed a kidney transplant. I interviewed him while he was on dialysis and we covered the successful transplant surgery of his brother's donated kidney. Afterwards he looked healthy and happy saying into the camera, "A great day is being able to pee."

I also did a series of reports on colon cancer when WYFF was giving away free colo-rectal tests. Later, a viewer wrote to tell me one of those kits saved his life when he discovered early that he was in the first stages of colon cancer. Thank-you's like that are priceless.

Another favorite story was about Kelly, a young girl who donated much of her time visiting and entertaining elderly patients in nursing homes. I recently ran across an old *TV Guide* ad I'd saved about that story and called her mother. Kelly grew up and got her nursing degree. And she and I are now friends on Facebook.

I've heard from many former colleagues and viewers through social media. Thank goodness Al Gore invented the Internet! (Although he never actually claimed to have done that.)

Getting Personal

Two of my most personal stories were health related. At WSPA I did a series looking at different types of stress-relieving techniques, including bio-feedback, exercise, and prayer.

I interviewed the director of the bio-feedback lab at an area university. As part of the story, I was taped doing Transcendental Meditation while hooked up to intimidating equipment that measured my heart rate, breathing, and galvanic skin response.

I was self-conscious and nervous and figured the results wouldn't even come close to all the scientific research I'd seen on TM. But after twenty minutes, the director looked at my results and said she'd never seen anyone get so deeply relaxed so quickly before. I asked if she'd ever measured anyone doing TM. She said no. I said, "Well, there you are."

That was the second most personally gratifying story I ever did. See page 35 for the first.

I did another related series at WYFF on Ayurvedic medicine, introduced in America by Maharishi Mahesh Yogi, who brought TM to the Western world.

The highlight of that assignment was interviewing Dr. Deepak Chopra at a time when the only people who'd heard of him were TM meditators. Chopra was originally head of Maharishi's Ayurvedic Association in North America before he went out on his own.

After I left television, I interviewed Maharishi himself over the telephone on Christmas Day, 1991. I can't describe the feeling of bliss and peace I felt after talking with him. That feeling is called "darshan" in the East Indian tradition. It's the raising of consciousness one gets in the presence of an enlightened being.

More Down to Earth Celebs

Many of my favorite assignments involved interviewing celebrities. I once did a series on The Marshall Tucker Band for WSPA. Great guys. Later I had the sad duty of writing and reporting on the death of one of its members, Tommy Caldwell, who was killed in a car accident. His parents wrote me a note, thanking me for doing such a good story about him.

The President Said it, Not Me

One complaint the management of WSPA got about me actually pleased me as a testament to my ability not to show my personal bias in my reporting.

Scott had written a story for the 11:00 newscast on President Reagan's State of the Union address. Scott chose a sound bite of the president saying scary things about possible cuts in Social Security.

Even though we usually wrote our own "voice-overs and readers," I ended up reading that story on the air. A viewer wrote to our Program Director complaining about my (Scott's) choice of the sound bite, saying the president had said more positive things in his speech that we should have focused on.

The letter said, "I don't know if Ms. Estes is a Republican or Democrat, but she should give credit where credit's due."

First of all, it's not a reporter's job to credit or discredit the president, but to report facts. Happily, I felt if this viewer couldn't tell after my several years of anchoring which political party I favored, then I must be doing something right.

Flying High

When I first joined the news team at WYFF, the station sent me to Rhein-Main Air Base in Germany to do a piece on our local Reserves stationed there. That was a treat.

Except there can't be a colder place on earth than Germany in March. (Not even winter in Iowa; although our winter this year was worse than Winterfell's!) The snow piles in Germany looked odd when the story aired in July when I began my anchor duties.

The highlight of that assignment was riding in the cockpit of a C-130 transport plane. On the trip home, the pilot let me call my mother in Arkansas on the cockpit's phone to tell her I was about to land in Greenland.

My Most Favorite Interview

Speaking of Mom, she was an integral part of my #1 favorite assignment at WSPA. For years growing up I'd heard of our family's ancestral home in a town near where I was living. I called the retired doctor and his wife who owned the home and they consented to let me do a story on it.

My mom came to visit and we toured the home built by her great-grandfather. She'd given me family photos of him; his oldest son, her grandfather; and *his* oldest son, her father.

I faded from one portrait to the other ending with a live close-up of "his oldest child, my mother" sitting in one of the rooms. She was enthralled to be there and gave me a very good interview.

She later compiled a family history, which one of her sisters printed and had copies bound for everyone on Mother's side of the family.

My Most Fun Story

Obviously, a lot of my work in TV was fun. You know you have a great job when you enjoy it so much, you'd almost do it for free. (Oh, I did that.)

One assignment WSPA gave me was pure fun. The Ritz-Carlton hotel in Atlanta invited broadcasters to spend a weekend at the hotel learning to cook gourmet dishes from their head chef. It was great PR for the hotel and a unique adventure for us.

Our news producer and his wife were gourmet cooks and convinced the station to send them along with me to do the story.

We learned to create some fabulous dishes and, of course, taped the process and interviews. I ended my story with a montage of shots from the weekend to the tune of "Puttin' on the Ritz."

Love the song, loved the food, loved the lessons. Staying at the Ritz-Carlton wasn't so bad, either.

More Celebrities

One of my most exciting adventures was covering the actors' strike in Hollywood in 1980. I was on vacation visiting an actor friend and WSPA asked me to do the strike story. I interviewed a number of CBS stars in the picket line. The station made arrangements for me to borrow a photographer from the network affiliate in Los Angeles, KCBS, and edit my story there.

My actor friend happened to be very active in the Screen Actors Guild union. He gave me a detail about the actors' demands no one else had reported involving compensation for Pay TV movies. The KCBS correspondent who covered the story for the network read my story and asked, "Is that really true?" I told him a reliable source in SAG had given me that information.

KCBS sent my story to WSPA on its linefeed. I watched the network coverage that evening. The correspondent included the information he'd gotten from me in his story.

Pretty cool. Always glad to help out a colleague; but so much for my "scoop." I feel sure he checked it out with SAG before taking my word for it.

Speaking of actors, I must confess that meeting and interviewing celebrities was my favorite part of being a local TV news anchor. I felt I did well treating them as regular folks even when star struck by meeting someone like Anthony Hopkins or James Earl Jones.

Want to hear some good stories about some of them? Turn the page.

6

Seeing Stars

Most of the TV and film celebrities I met were from CBS-TV special programs and series. CBS would host "Star Weekends" twice a year at a posh hotel – summers in Atlanta and winters in Los Angeles. WSPA sent me to do promos and interviews with the network stars.

My best friend, Sherry, sometimes went with me to rub elbows with them. In 1980, on the way to Atlanta I was looking through the packet the network sent us, which included the stars' photos, bios, and synopses of their shows. I told Sherry and our morning show hostess at the time that they could have anyone they wanted except for Tom Selleck. He was mine! (Right.) I'd only seen him on TV doing his Salem cigarette commercials. He was coming to Atlanta to promote his new show, *Magnum, P.I.*

I interviewed him; he's as nice as he seems. In the evening when the taping of interviews and promos had ended for the day, Sherry and I were in the hospitality suite posing to have our picture taken with Eric Scott (Ben of *The Waltons*). I noticed Selleck standing across the room smiling at us. I quizzically motioned asking if he wanted to be in the photo and he nodded, "Yes." So, he joined us. You can be sure my photo with just the two of us is framed and sitting on my office bookshelf.

The Men

When I would ask the male celebrities to autograph their 8X10 glossies, I'd say, "Write something that will make my boyfriend jealous." And they accommodated.

Selleck wrote, *"I'll never forget that day in the suite."* (Uh, we did the interviews in a hotel suite.)

Similar to Bill Bixby (*The Incredible Hulk*), who signed, *"What fun we had in that Los Angeles hotel. Many thanks."* (No, thank *you*.)

Ken Howard (*The White Shadow*): *"Fun working and playing together!!!* (I *wish*.)

Ron Leibman (*Kaz*): *"Good lookin' news broad."* (Sexist, but who cares?)

And my favorite along these lines:

"I love you and hope to see you again." John Schneider (*The Dukes of Hazzard*).

John, if you're reading this, I'm still waiting.

Some of my favorites, professionally speaking:

"For Annette Estes, who has the talent to make the bad news seem good." Lou Holtz (Head Football Coach, Arkansas)

"Best wishes to a dedicated and able journalist, Annette Estes." Sen. Strom Thurmond (R-SC).

"Annette, I couldn't have done it without you!" John Houseman (*The Paper Chase*). Okay, I asked him to write that, but still.

I've always thought I should own a Sardis-type restaurant and put all my autographed photos on the walls.

The Women

I was just as pleased to interview my favorite female stars.

Linda Gray (*Dallas*) wrote, *"I loved working with you! With love and thanks."*

Mary Frann (*Newhart*): *"For Annette – a beautiful, brainy interview."*

Joan Van Ark (*Knot's Landing*): *"To Annette – You're great!"*

Happy Birthday to Us

One star is the only person I ever met who was born on exactly the same day I was – Bonnie Franklin (*One Day at a Time*). Franklin's bio listed her birthday – January 6th (sans the year; women worried about that sort of thing before the Internet revealed all). During our interview I mentioned we had the same birthday and she asked, "What year?" I said, "You first." She told me and I exclaimed, "Me, too!" So, we were born in the same month, same year, and on the same day. Maybe even the same time, although she couldn't recall her time of birth. Unlike mine, her mother didn't tell her.

She autographed her photo to me, *"Annette, Happy Birthday. You were born on a terrific day!!"* And our interview was in LA in January, just a few days after our birthdays.

I was sad when she died in 2013. I always felt a special kinship with her.

So now if you want to know my age, just Google Bonnie and you'll know. I don't mind. Every birthday I thank God for another year of life.

Nights on the Towns

In 1979 in Atlanta, my friend Sherry and I went to the hospitality suite the evening we arrived. We immediately recognized Vic Tayback (*Alice*) sitting with a man who looked familiar, but we didn't recognize. He turned out to be Brian Dennehy, there to promote his new show *Big Shamus, Little Shamus* which, unfortunately, didn't survive for long. Fortunately, he has!

We all got to talking and Vic said we should show them the town. We took them to the Polaris Lounge and got off the elevator to be greeted by a huge ice sculpture that was carved "Toshiba." At that moment a horde of Japanese men came rushing up to us shouting. "MEL! It's MEL!" Vic graciously signed autographs and posed for pictures while the rest of us blended into the wallpaper.

The next day I interviewed Vic and Brian. They autographed their photos to me:

Vic: *"Annette – you made me remember Atlanta!! You're an absolute doll!!*

Brian: *"Annette – a terrific lady!"*

Thanks, guys.

The following January, Sherry went along with me to the LA Star Weekend where we saw Vic again and he invited us and my crew to dinner. It was a fun evening. That was the last time we saw him. I felt I'd lost a friend when he died in 1990.

Thanks, Whoever Shot J.R.

Fans of the original *Dallas* show will remember the summer of 1979 when all we talked about was the greatest cliffhanger of all times – who shot J.R.? That summer Ken Kercheval (a likely suspect, Cliff Barnes) attended the Atlanta Star Weekend. I had an idea for a promo we could shoot and pitched it to our promotion director. She liked it and Kercheval did, too.

As our camera rolled, he was standing alone looking worried, devious, and puzzled all at the same time. I rushed up to him with my Eyewitness News microphone and "interviewed" him to get the scoop on who shot JR?

He told me he didn't know. (Or did he?) I pressed him, but he wouldn't tell me. So, I signed off saying we'll just have to wait until September to find out.

Our station – and I – both won local ADDY's (American Advertising Awards) for the spot, which I proudly display in my office and on my website. We found out in Season 3 that it was Sue Ellen's sister, Kristin Shepard, who shot J.R. But wasn't it fun speculating that summer?

Thanks, Larry Hagman, for all those years of loving/hating you. We miss you.

Grease Is the Word!

I had a fun encounter with one TV actor I interviewed in LA. He was a cast member of the short-lived CBS show *Flatbush* and many others (*Happy Days, CHiPs and more*). His name is Randy Stumpf.

Months later WSPA sent me to New York to do promos and interview CBS newscasters. From the hospitality suite window (I spent a lot of time in those) that night I noticed a Klieg light doing its thing in front of the hotel. Naturally, "dedicated and able journalist" I was, I had to go to the lobby to see what the excitement was all about. (Well, it could have been the president who'd give me an exclusive interview and I didn't want to get fired for missing it.) Alas, it was just a long line of people heading into the ballroom. But someone in the know told me it was every actor, singer, and dancer who'd ever been in the musical *Grease*, including the movie, celebrating because that night *Grease* had become the longest-ever running show on Broadway.

Who did I see in the line but Randy Stumpf. He recognized me and came over to say hello. I was behind the roped-off area for looky-loos, but Randy invited me to go in with him.

We were told that at the far end of the mammoth, crowded room was a roped-off area where John Travolta, Olivia Newton-John, Stockard Channing, etc. were seated, surrounded by security guards. I was on the wrong side of the rope again.

Randy did introduce me to Jeff Conaway (*Taxi*), who played Kenickie in the film.

Huge party. Nice party. Thanks, Randy.

I actually did anchor the news that year, even though it doesn't sound like it. I loved my anchor job but as I said earlier, interviewing celebrities was my favorite thing to do. Looking back, it was Oprah's job I really wanted. But for a while I had the best of both worlds. Interestingly, for a brief time in 1977, Oprah and I were both news anchors in different markets; she at WJZ in Baltimore.

Of course, my most favorite professional autograph: the person who signed my paychecks. Although, as we've established, I would have done this for free.

Stars, Novas, and Galaxies

Here are some of the celebrities I worked with who aren't mentioned or pictured elsewhere:

Alabama	Dean Jones
Bob Barker	Elaine Joyce
Bibi Besch	Stacy Keach
Ed Bradley	Michael Keaton
Eileen Brennan	Charles Kuralt
Rory Calhoun	Diane Ladd
Frank Capra	Michele Lee
Capt. Kangaroo	Peter Nero
Connie Chung	Sarah Jessica Parker
Tim Curry	Lynn Redgrave
Tyne Daly	Jerry Reed
Wayne Dyer	Wayne Rogers
Jamie Farr	Marc Singer
Sharon Gless	Susan Sullivan
Phyllis George	Loretta Swit
Alex Haley	Ralph Waite
Robert Hogan	Sam Waterston

I don't remember meeting my first movie star because I was around 2 years old. My dad told me about it. He played piano in a Navy band when stationed in San Diego.

He got a small part in a movie; don't know which one. At a cast party Dad tickled the ivories with Jimmy Stewart sitting on the bench next to him, as I sat in the actor's lap.

Gee, Dad, you could have had someone take a picture of us.

Some people I worked with in TV went on to become celebs.

Jane Robelot, reporter extraordinaire and one of my favorite people. She eventually moved way up to co-anchor the CBS Morning News. As of this writing she's back home, anchoring at WYFF.

Leeza Gibbons auditioned at WSPA when I had just begun anchoring. I happened to go to the control room for something and saw her being taped reading news scripts on the anchor desk. General Manager Vernon walked in, took one look at her and said "she's hired." He had a good eye for talent.

Leeza quickly became one of our market's favorite reporters. Later, our sports director Sam told me she'd asked his advice when she was offered a job on a talk show, *P.M. America*, for CBS Affiliate KDFM. He told her not to take the job because news was more prestigious and financially rewarding. She decided to do it anyway and the rest is history.

I feel sure she's been more "financially rewarded" than all the rest of us combined. And we never became a household name. Well done, Leeza!

7

Rumors, Rumors

An occupational hazard of being a television personality, whether national or local, is that viewers love to hear and spread rumors about you. I had my share, which I usually heard about from colleagues and friends. A few I heard directly; I gave a shocking response to one, which I'll share later.

Here are some rumors that went around about me; how and where they got started, I know not.

When I was in my early 30s there was a rumor that I was dating a teenager from a nearby small town. All I can figure out is that some teen from that town started the rumor himself.

But he wasn't alone. One night a woman came up to me in a restaurant bathroom and told me I had dated her uncle. I asked his name and had to disappoint her by saying I'd never heard of him. Now boys, it isn't nice to spread false rumors.

A woman who worked in our programming department at WSPA is the one I mentioned in Chapter Three who had done the weather years earlier. We were sad to learn that her boyfriend had died of a heart attack (rumors were he died in her bed, but I didn't ask when giving her my condolences).

Sure enough, the gossipmongers had it happening to *my* boyfriend in *my* bed. Of course, they did.

Most of the false stories I heard about myself amused me. One of them angered me for two reasons.

Since I was making good money as a news anchor, I bought a Cadillac El Dorado. I named her "Libby," because I felt if I could afford a Cadillac on my own, I was truly liberated.

But soon a fellow reporter came in from the field and told me what people were saying. Their version was that I was having an affair with a local business owner (again, never heard of him) and he bought me the car so I wouldn't tell his wife.

Okay, I didn't like it that people thought I was having an affair with a married man. That was bad enough. But what really ticked me off is that people thought I couldn't afford to buy a luxury car and had to sleep around to get one.

I suppose I was more professionally miffed than personally. Either way, shame on you people.

There were a couple of amusing items that involved products people buy. Once I was in a grocery store looking at hair products. I saw a bottle of Afro-Sheen on the shelf. I thought, well if it would make black people's hair shine maybe it would work on mine, too, so I bought it.

Not a week later the rumor was going around that I was living with a black man. Not that there's anything wrong with that, but I'm pretty sure that's how that rumor got started by a nosey cashier.

This one may be the best – or worst depending on your point of view.

The story goes that my boyfriend cheated on me and to get back at him I got some Super Glue and, well, glued his private parts together while he was sleeping. That is funny when you think about it. Dumb, but better than saying I'd set the mattress on fire and killed him.

For the record, neither one of those things is true. Enough with the rumors, already.

Although that does remind me of the most insidious lie someone told about me – not to their friends, but to the local sheriff.

Of course, I knew the sheriff so I wasn't upset when my phone rang and it was him. Until I heard why he was calling.

He said someone had called him and said I had murdered a man and buried him somewhere. Again, a name I'd never heard. I told the sheriff I wasn't guilty (which he pretty much knew but I suppose was legally obligated to follow up on the call) and said I hoped no one by that name turned up dead or I guess he'd be calling *on* me.

Fortunately, for the "victim," we never reported such a death on the news and I never heard back from the sheriff, so apparently there was no murder.

What kind of person does that sort of thing? Some people need to get a life. No pun intended.

If these rumors were true, I would have been too *tired* to do the news. There's another juicy one to relate, actually more of a misunderstanding. Be patient, that comes later.

The main life lesson I learned from all this is that I never believe any gossip I hear about anyone unless they tell me themselves. Good lesson.

8
Bloops and Bleeps

Everyone loves it when broadcasters mess up and something goes out over the air that wasn't supposed to be seen or heard.

Everyone except the ones who do it.

But we all love outtakes and screw-ups, so I hope you enjoy hearing about the following. I wish I could remember them all.

We know rookies make mistakes and I was no exception. My first weekend anchoring the news was thrilling, but I was extremely nervous. I'm not sure it showed physically but my tongue sure got twisted. It started at the beginning when I said, "Good evening," and then couldn't pronounce my own name. I got it right on the second try, but I believe I fluffed words in every story.

I felt really frustrated after the newscast and figured they wondered why they ever hired me. I wondered myself.

Jack, the weekend sports anchor, had called the news director at home and told him how bad I was feeling. The news director called me later as I was writing the 11:00 newscast. He started "chewing me out" saying how could I *do* that.

But he was joking and told me I did fine and not to worry about it. Just go on and do better at 11:00. I did and it all worked out okay.

That's not to say I never got my tongue tied again, but I learned to laugh at myself. When you can do that, people don't mind; they laugh with you.

My co-anchor Scott was reporting on a meeting of the NAACP. He got ahead of himself and instead of saying "N-double-A-CP leaders" he said "N-double-A-C Peters."

"No way," he said when we told him. Often, we don't realize when we've made such a blunder. But he watched the show tape and had to admit it. He laughed along with us.

That might have been a bit raunchy, but my next one was really dumb. I was announcing the selection of the new pope, John Paul. Instead of informing the viewers he was the first Polish pope, I told them he was the first Catholic pope. What was I thinking?

Once our hippy-dippy weatherman, James, had to report on tornadoes moving toward parts of our viewing area. Trying to reassure the viewers, he told them not to worry, that it would happen while they were asleep. I'm sure they felt much better then.

That reminds me of something I did at WLKY. One afternoon there was a tornado warning and I was corralled to make a voice-over announcement. I was petrified at the idea of tornadoes bearing down on us and I'm sure I scared the viewers with the panic in my voice.

If only *they'd* been asleep.

It's not only on-air talent that makes mistakes. One of our worst ones at WSPA was done by the person who typed the "supers" that would appear on the screen under someone's "talking head."

The reporter was interviewing an administrator with the School for the Deaf and Blind in our area. Under his name the super read, "School for the Deaf and Dumb." *Really* bad. I cringe again just writing this.

This isn't a blooper, but an amusing story. WSPA was in search of a new weatherman. Our general manager, Vernon, and his staff looked at a lot of demo tapes from forecasters around the country. Some apparently were pretty goofy.

Vernon told some of us after deciding to hire Jerry that as someone was putting his demo tape into the VCR, he hoped this would be a good one. As they pushed the Play button, he added, "We're not going to hire some clown!"

Up on the screen popped Jerry. Doing the weather. In a clown suit.

But he was personable and originally from our area, so he was hired. He eventually became one of the most popular personalities in the market.

In fact, a few years ago as of this writing, I heard the station forced him into retirement. I understand viewers complained so strongly they hired him back.

Way to go, Jerry!

Even management must learn to never say never.

9

It's Too Hot to F***?

Okay, this is the big one. The most inglorious moment of my career. This is what happened as I remember it. And how could I ever forget?

A Hot Wednesday in July, 1986

I came to work early because I was working on a special series. I'd been out in a news car all afternoon with my photographer, Tim. The car's air conditioner wasn't working and it was miserably hot.

WSPA had just rehired a news director we'd had several years past. Harry was an impatient, controlling sort who had no qualms about chewing someone out in front of everyone in the newsroom.

Tim asked as we rode along, did I think there was a lot more tension among the troops since he'd returned. We agreed there was and complained, as employees are wont to do.

So, I got back to the station feeling hot, tired, and grumpy. This is not to make excuses, but to explain my state of mind and set the scene for what would happen during the newscast.

I am the type of person who speaks her mind whether I

should or not. My motto: "Everyone's entitled to my opinion." And, although it's hard to admit, I can be judgmental when I feel people aren't doing the job they're being paid to do.

(Maybe that's partly why I'm now a consultant specializing in helping companies hire and manage the right people to achieve superior employee job performance.)

News Time

At 5:55 P.M. Brad and I had settled into our anchor seats for the day's early evening edition of Eyewitness News. Everything was running along smoothly until we threw it to our weatherman, Gene.

We noticed our floor manager (the one who gave us our on-air cues) was crawling on the floor toward Gene motioning for him to take off his mic and hand it down. I knew that meant Gene's mic wasn't working.

The thought went through my mind that it was the studio crew's job to make sure the cameras, lights, microphones, and monitors were working before each newscast. So, it appeared to me that someone hadn't done his job.

I turned to Brad and whispered, *"Why don't they check the f***ing mics?!"*

A few moments later the producer spoke into our earpieces for us not to say anything because my mic was open full to pick up what Gene was saying.

We gave thumbs up and nodded, "O.K." Too late.

They finally got his mic working; he finished the forecast and we went to commercials. During the break the news director, Harry, opened the studio door and said we were getting calls that someone had said the "F" word on the air. We said "Nuh-uh." Like Scott before, I had no recollection of having said it.

After the newscast as I returned to the newsroom, Harry said, "Follow me." He took me to a booth, played back the show tape and there it was.

Barely audible, but there none the less.

My heart fell to my stomach and my entire career flashed in front of my eyes.

Now What?

The news director usually went home after the 6:00 P.M. newscast and upper management before then. Harry didn't go home and the others returned. There was no hole for me to crawl into.

They decided not to fire me (whew!). Harry told me to write an apology for him to approve, which would be recorded to run before the 11:00 P.M. news that night and the 6:00 P.M. news the following day.

So, I did.

To Harry's credit, he was sensitive about my feelings and didn't criticize me.

Now Everyone Knows

The next day the switchboard operator told me they only got a few calls. But after my apology aired twice, everybody in the viewing area knew what I'd done even if they didn't know exactly what I'd said.

Everyone with a voice to be heard had their opinion. The morning radio personalities had a field day. I didn't listen to them but heard about it.

The print media got into the act from the largest daily

paper to the smallest weekly. One columnist's headline read, "First Santa Claus, then the Easter Bunny, now Annette."

Well, at least I was in good company. But I don't recall either of them ever saying the "F" word.

The mail came pouring in. Management decided the newsroom secretary would read everything addressed to me and give me only the positive letters.

I got a lot of support from viewers. I still have in my office a cardboard fan that says on the front: "I'm an Annette Estes fan." On the back a group of women had signed their names and written comments of their support. Some said the fan was to help me "keep my cool."

One afternoon I passed the general manager's secretary in the hall and apologized profusely to her. I figured it had made a lot of extra work for her answering calls and letters. She said not to worry, that 90% of the reactions were positive.

Wow, that made me feel a lot better.

Wake Up Call

Eventually, as with everything, we moved on to more important matters. But what I'd done had a profound effect on me.

I became the nicest, sweetest, most cooperative person in the newsroom. I realized I'd dodged a bullet and needed to clean up my act. And I wasn't acting. This was a truly humbling experience for me and the changes I made were real and sincere.

A few weeks later the newsroom secretary called me a "Pollyanna." She meant it. Best compliment I've ever gotten.

By the way, the only other person who got reprimanded for my blunder was the young woman who ran the audio board. To my knowledge, no one ever said anything to the men who directed and produced the show and made the decision to open my mic. Just saying. Still, the fault was all mine.

Contract Renewal Time

Fast forward to October. My contract was up the end of December and they always started negotiations three months in advance.

I had been at WSPA for ten years. At some point I'd decided I needed to move on. The general manager refused to negotiate with agents, but I got one anyway.

Our meteorologist, Jerry, was on board at that time (sans the clown suit) and he told me about Don, an excellent agent in San Francisco. I hired him and am so glad I did.

Don helped me enormously behind the scenes in my negotiations with Harry. He gave me confidence that, as it turns out, I *really* needed.

And he did a whole lot more.

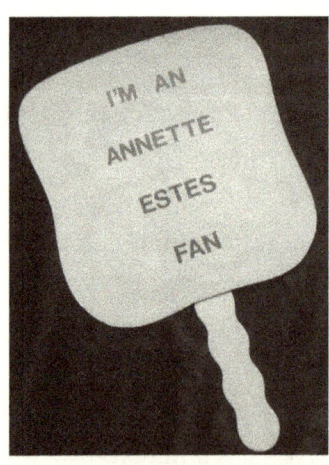

10

The Fallout

Before I tell you how my contract talks went, I want to mention one person's response which meant the world to me.

A few years earlier, my best friend Sherry and I had a falling out that ended our friendship. The night after "Black Wednesday" (as I call it), I got home and there was a gift bag hanging on my front door knob. Inside were a small stuffed teddy bear and a card that read on the front: "*There's a word for people who act like you…*"

Inside: "*FRIEND. And I'm glad you're mine.*"

Sherry

And we were friends again. Something good always comes from a bad situation.

The best response came from my mother. That comes later.

Nice Try

The first night I met with Harry in his office to talk about my contract he began with this statement:

"Vernon (the general manager, whom up until now used

to lead the negotiations himself) thought about not renewing your contract because of what happened in July. Then he decided we would sign you to another year's contract at the same pay."

With the exception of the $10,000 raise I got when Scott left, I'd usually get a salary increase of $2,000 no matter what I asked for. So, I wasn't expecting much, but this was unacceptable.

I said, "Harry, I know what I did was awful for the station. It was awful for me. But I apologized, and it's in the past now.

"So, if that's going to be a condition of our negotiations, we have nothing to talk about."

He said, "You're right." And he never mentioned it again.

My agent was proud of me. I was, too.

Secret Agent

At our next meeting as I sat down Harry began by saying, "We hear you have an agent."

"Yes."

He didn't ask who my agent was, so I didn't tell him. If he'd asked, I would have told him it was Don.

At the time I was dating Terry. Our third meeting began with Harry speculating, "We think Terry is your agent."

I smiled and said, "No, Terry is very intelligent and gives me good advice, but he's not my agent."

He still didn't ask who my agent was and I still didn't tell him.

The station was offering a $2,000 raise by this time. But Christmas vacation was coming up, so I told them I'd give them my answer before the end of the year.

Agent's Secret

One weekend I flew to San Francisco to meet Don and discuss negotiation strategy. He knew I wanted a higher paying job in another market. He said he'd work on that. But fate had other plans.

It was, and I guess still is, a common practice among local television stations for one news department to send out demo tapes of a news anchor at a competing station in hopes of getting that anchor out of the market.

Don contacted the general manager of WYFF, the NBC affiliate in our market, to see if they'd like to help him find me a job in another market.

Their response was, "We'd be interested in talking with you about hiring her ourselves."

I said go for it and our negotiations with WYFF began.

They worked with Don and drew up a contract he thought was good. Terry and I (everybody knew and liked him) met with WYFF's general manager and station manager to talk terms.

Usually one has to go to a bigger market to get a significant increase in salary, but not this time. Now I'm going to reveal what I was making at WSPA and what WYFF offered me. Since that was in 1986, I suppose it doesn't matter now.

Although in 1984, a writer for *Woman's Day* magazine contacted me. Barbara Bartocci was writing an article entitled *Pushing Upstream: Succeeding Against the Odds*. *Pushing* was the stories of five women who succeeded in careers for which they had little or no training. (Yeah, it's hanging on my wall.)

Ms. Bartocci included my story in her article and asked me what my salary was. I knew WSPA would not want me to reveal that so I didn't. I told her I made between $40,000 and $70,000. When her article was published it stated that I made $50,000 a year, which was right on the money. (Again, with the puns.)

GM Vernon was not happy with me and let me know it, but I told him what I'd told the author and that she'd made an accurate lucky guess, or found out some other way. I suppose he believed me.

But I digress.

An Offer I Maybe Couldn't Refuse

In 1986, I was making $60,000 a year at WSPA, with a pending $2,000 raise at the time. No perks, except I did negotiate an extra two-week's vacation once in lieu of money, which I continued to get.

Here's what WYFF offered me:
- A five-year contract
- $75,000 in 1987
- $80,000 in 1988
- $85,000 in 1989
- $90,000 in 1990
- $100, 000 in 1991
- $300 a month clothing allowance
- $300 a month car allowance

I can live with that. However, I had to think about it – in part because of WSPA's pension plan, which I was told has since been made illegal.

WSPA would set aside money for employees each year; the employees contributed nothing. At the end of fifteen years I would have been fully vested in the plan. At ten years, I had accumulated $86,000, which I would receive in full if I left.

One contingency in my contract was that if I were to be offered a job in the same market, I was required to give WSPA an opportunity to meet or exceed the offer.

And there was some loyalty to WSPA in the mix.

Home for Christmas

So, I had a lot to think about over the holidays. Our noon anchor, Joan, was a good and trusted friend, who knew I might be leaving. I gave her my mother's phone number and told her to call me if she heard any scuttlebutt while I was on vacation.

I hadn't told my mother yet what had happened in July because I wanted to tell her in person. She may have already known because one of her sisters and her husband had friends in my area. But if any of them knew beforehand, they never told me.

I remember my mother and I were lying on her bed as I told her what I've told you so far. I told her some of the negative reactions and how the station had thrown it in my face at the beginning of our contract talks. Her response to that was, "Well, F*** them!"

My sweet, proper mother had probably never uttered that word before – or since. You can imagine how much I loved and appreciated her at that moment. I am so blessed to have had such a wonderful mother. She lived with me for the last twelve years of her life. She died in 2011 at age 99. I miss and think of her every day.

Joan did call me once to say Sam, the sports anchor, had mentioned something about my situation, but I don't remember what it was.

Decision Time

When I returned home from vacation, I'd decided to accept WYFF's offer if WSPA didn't meet or beat it. I called Vernon and told him I wanted to come in and talk with him. He asked what it was about and I said I'd tell him when we met that afternoon.

I called Harry, told him I was meeting with Vernon, and said it was fine with me if he wanted to be at the meeting, too.

My agent, Don, had written Vernon a letter stating the terms of the offer I'd received. He wasn't obligated under the terms of my contract to tell him what station had made the offer.

Also, he didn't tell them my exact salary offer, just the percentage of increases; plus the car and clothing allowances.

It was a great letter. Don was worth every penny of the 7% of my salary he'd earn each year.

I don't know what I would have done if Vernon had matched or bettered WYFF's offer. But he made it easy for me.

He tossed the letter back to me and said, "I guess you've priced yourself out of this market." I managed to keep a straight face, and confirmed he wouldn't meet or beat the offer. Nope. I said okay, then, I'd be leaving.

Harry sat on the couch and said nothing. Vernon asked me where I was going. I looked him straight in the eye and said, "Not far."

Later Harry told me they called every station in nearby states to find out who hired me. They never guessed where I was going.

I left Vernon's office and met Joan in the women's restroom. As she already knew I would probably be leaving, I confirmed it.

I told her Vernon had asked me to come back for two weeks while they searched for my replacement. I asked her to let me know if she heard anything before my vacation was over.

Imagine my surprise – and undying gratitude – when she did.

Annette and Mom

11

Moving On

Vacation's over.
 Time to go back and give WSPA the two weeks I'd promised them.

Best Birthday Ever!

I was due back on January 6th, my birthday, you remember. As I was getting ready, Joan called me with the news that WSPA wanted *her* to fill my anchor seat.

She went on to say they were going to announce my leaving and her promotion at a special meeting of the news staff that evening after the newscast at 6:30.

Joan knew I was going across the street, so to speak, and knew we'd be rivals for ratings now. She earnestly said if that would hurt our friendship, she wouldn't take the job. I told her to let management worry about the ratings and that it wouldn't affect our friendship as far as I was concerned.

Since she later went on to work for a national network, I've always wondered what would have happened if I'd said it *would* hurt our friendship. ☺

I hung up and immediately called WYFF's promotion

Moving On

director, Janet (whom I'd also worked with at WSPA). Later that afternoon, I got a call from WYFF's station manager, Bob, who told me what had ensued when they sprang into action:

- They met with Karen, the anchor I was going to replace at 6:00 and 11:00. She was given the noon anchor job and the health reporter beat. She knew it was a possibility and took it well. We got along well during my time there and are now Facebook friends.

- They prepared a press release to send the newspapers but didn't submit them just yet.

- They knew WSPA's news meeting wouldn't begin until 6:30. WYFF's newscast ran an hour from 6:00 to 7:00. Just before the 6:30 break, the anchor I would be joining would announce that I was coming to WYFF. So, they would beat WSPA's announcement to the staff by letting the entire viewing audience know.

Then Bob told me he had called Vernon late that afternoon to say, "We hear Annette's leaving." He told me Vernon said, "No one's supposed to know that." Bob told him, "What you don't know, Vernon, is that Annette is coming to work for us."

I wish I'd been a fly on the wall. Vernon reminded him that my contract stated if I went to a station in the same market, I couldn't be on the air for six months. Bob said WYFF intended to honor that stipulation.

I watched WYFF's newscast that night and heard Kent telling the viewers I'd be joining him the first of July.

I was to begin working in January, but took the month off to find a house in WYFF's town. It's ironic that I'd been wanting to move there anyway.

Time to change the channel.

WYFF promotes itself as "We're Your Friend Four."

One day I went to the WSPA newsroom for the last time to clean out my desk.

As I was packing my things while people were working, sports anchor Jack burst through the doors and loudly informed us that, "Now we know what WYFF really stands for – We're Your F***ing Friend!"

I tried hard to look offended, but was too busy laughing along with everyone else.

Months before all this happened, Joan and I had made a pact that whoever left WSPA first would take the other to dinner at a restaurant of her choice. I felt sure she would leave first, but we went for a steak dinner at a fine restaurant – my treat.

We had fun.

So, for all of you who believed the rumor that WSPA fired me, now you know the truth. I mean, c'mon, if they were going to fire me, they would have done it when it happened, not five months later. They wanted me to stay, just not enough to pay me what WYFF was offering.

Oh, just to let you know. Vernon asked me recently to be his Facebook friend and I said yes. All's well that ends well.

12
Changing Channels

So here I was – same time, different station.
Since I couldn't be on-air for another five months, I had it pretty easy. I'd do some writing and help out in any way I could. It was kind of like being an intern again. I felt like I was being way over-paid. Not complaining.

WYFF toyed with the idea of putting me in the anchor seat anyway and ignoring WSPA's contract. But they decided against it, I suppose because then everyone else could violate their contracts.

At times during the newscast, part of the newsroom could be seen. I *sooo* wanted to walk across the shot in the background, but thought better of it.

Another *Really* Black Wednesday

My first night on the air was Wednesday, July 1, 1987. I came in with a bang. We were set up outside at a big festival and thunderstorms were on their way. We braved the rain under a canopy that was about to collapse until a lightning strike that caused our earpieces and microphones to buzz. When that happened, our meteorologist, Chuck, tore off his mic and walked away grumbling, "I'm not getting paid enough to get electrocuted." Hear, hear!

The decision was made to finish the newscast in the studio with noon anchors Kevin and Karen and we all packed up and left for dryer ground.

A harbinger of things to come?

Before I came to work at WYFF, the general manager, Drew, wrote me a wise letter. He cautioned me that not everyone at WYFF would be happy that I was joining them and I needed to be prepared and win them over. He was right. Although I didn't win everyone over.

Many viewers over the years told me they followed me to watch WYFF's news. That was nice.

I figured if Karen, whom I'd replaced on the anchor desk, was all right with it everyone else should be. But not everyone had the maturity and graciousness she did.

Déjà-vu, Sort of

I've already told you some of the things that happened at WYFF. Most of the time everything was fine. I got along well with my co-anchor Kent, who was a sweetheart and a gentleman whom everyone loved. But even his endorsement wasn't enough for some of my new co-workers.

One of my detractors was Mac, the aforementioned director of the dirty jokes. I must have murdered his mother in a former life because he had no use for me and getting along with him was hopeless.

One "battle" during a newscast he definitely won.

One night during the 6:00 news a new cameraman had pulled his camera too close to the set so that when Kent was on camera my hair would get in the shot when I looked down to follow the script. Mac yelled into my earpiece (talking to the floor manager) to tell me to get out of the shot.

During a video I explained that the camera was actually touching the set and I couldn't help it; that the camera needed to be moved.

Made no difference to him. He yelled, "Tell her if she doesn't get her hair out of the shot, I'm going to come down there and cut it off!"

I lost it. I looked into the camera and said, "You tell him to go…" I knew what I was about to say, but I couldn't stop myself. So, I put my hand over my mouth and said "go… *HMM*-hmm-hmm."

If the camera had come on me at that moment, the viewers would have heard me mumbling something unintelligible into my hand and would have had a good laugh.

But Mac complained to management and I was called in the next day to a big pow-wow. Here I was in the principal's office again being chastised like a 3rd grader.

I pointed out to them that I said nothing offensive from the news desk and shouldn't I get points for covering my mouth. I'd learned my lesson. For all anyone knew I could have said, "Tell him to go take a hike."

But they wouldn't listen. I was sentenced to three days off without pay.

You're OK, I'm not OK

Skip ahead a few months. Kent was off and our noon anchor Kevin was filling in.

During the 6:00 newscast the teleprompter operator lost his place while Kevin was introducing a story. He got a little tongue-twisted and had to finish reading from his hard copy of the script.

During the story video, Kevin let loose with a litany of foul language directed at the poor teleprompter guy, including the infamous "F" word and worse:

"You m-effing, GD, SOB; you effing a-hole….and on and on." He was so loud viewers could have heard him even without a microphone.

All I could think of was how he was going to get lectured and have three days off without pay.

What management did to him was…

Nothing.

I'll always wonder why.

Out of Focus

One of my shortcomings got me in trouble more than once. But I found a solution.

Kent and I took turns each day doing two live 30-second "teases" for the upcoming newscast. A camera was set up in the newsroom for us to do the promo for the stories we were covering that day.

I don't know how Kent did it, but invariably I'd be so focused on writing stories I'd lose track of time and miss my turn. Viewers got to see 30-seconds of people working and walking around the newsroom.

I have a tendency to get absorbed in what I'm doing and not watch the clock. And of course, Mac (the aspiring hairdresser who was going to cut off my hair) wasn't about to remind me over the newsroom intercom that it was almost time to do the cut-in. He'd rather make the whole newsroom look bad along with me. So much for teamwork.

My solution was simple. I got an alarm clock and set it for

five minutes before time. Problem solved. (I still have to set an alarm before I'm supposed to do something at an appointed time.)

One thing that used to bug me was the content of those teases. What would happen is the assignment editor would give a reporter a story to cover. Based on the information given to her, she would write the tease for us to deliver.

But when the reporter got back, the story was different than we'd teased. I'd see it on the news monitor when it aired and felt I should apologize to the viewers for misleading them earlier in the day.

I used to think, *"we're in the communications business, yet we can't communicate with each other across the room."* I was probably the only person bothered by that.

Thinking of focusing reminds me of being punked when I was first hired back at WSPA. An engineer asked me to go get some focusing fluid for the studio cameras. That sounded weird and made me suspicious. I don't remember if I did it or not, but apparently that was a standard joke played on new hires.

Play it Again, Sam

One day WYFF's general manager, Drew, called me in to give me some news. He told me WYFF had decided to hire Sam, the sports anchor at WSPA. Oh, no, getting away from his criticism was one of the bonuses of leaving WSPA.

But he was really good and hard-working and I understood why WYFF wanted him. So, I called Sam at WSPA to congratulate him and said I knew we'd had our problems in the past, but this was a great station to work for and I hoped we could get along better here.

And we did.

NBC Junkets

One thing I missed at WYFF was the CBS Star Weekends. I did get to interview some celebrities who came to our town, Dinah Shore, Garrison Keillor, Steven Nichols (Patch) and Charles Shaughnessy (Shane Donovan) from *Days of Our Lives*.

I was a big *Days* fan. Many superstars began their careers on the daytime shows. And now, popular film actors are starring in prime-time TV shows. And we reap the benefits.

WYFF would send us to New York to do promos with the NBC newscasters, notably Tom Brokaw. And they'd let us stay over to eat at fine restaurants and see Broadway shows. That was the first time I saw *CATS*.

Jump ahead about eighteen years. Brokaw came to our town to cover the presidential race. I was attending a gathering and when I heard he'd be there, I grabbed a photo of the two of us taken back then. He'd never autographed it, so I figured it was high time. When I gave it to him to sign, he groaned that we both looked like children.

Well, at least we're wiser now. I guess.

The New General Manager

Our GM Drew, one of my favorite people of all times (as are his son and daughter-in-law, local actors in town), retired. His replacement made WSPA's news director Harry look like Mr. Rogers.

Apparently, Dick was hired to make big budget cuts, which meant axing highly-paid, mostly aging department heads and on-air personalities.

Things got tense, everyone wondering who'd be next.

The first anchor to go was Chuck, our meteorologist. But he was past retirement age, so it wasn't too unexpected.

Dick decided that we (he?) needed better security at the station, so he had coded keypads installed for employees to enter the building. It would be changed every time someone left, which was happening more and more frequently.

But we continued to do our jobs and get good ratings.

Signing Off

Eventually it was October, 1991, the last three months before my five-year contract expired. The executives who'd hired me had left the station. My agent Don kept trying to reach the news director, Allen, to begin negotiations, but Allen would never call him back. Didn't need a teleprompter to see the writing on the wall.

When I got to work on Friday, December 6th, Allen asked me to go with him to Dick's office, where they told me they weren't going to renew my contract. When I asked why, Dick said it was because I "didn't fit the direction they were going in the 90s." Whatever that meant.

During the meeting a beaded necklace I was wearing decided to break and the three of us spent some time picking beads up off the floor. That was awkward, but on a TV sitcom it would have been comic relief.

As Allen walked me back to my desk (where my 500 new business cards were still sitting after having been delivered a week before), he said – and I kid you not – "So, Annette, how has your day been?"

Really?

I said, "Oh fine, Allen, just fine."

The only person in the newsroom (just a few were there,

most had scattered) who would look me in the eye was Kent. He walked me to my car saying he was worried now, that he'd be next.

That night Karen had her job back, so they were back to where they were in the 80s.

Karen called me to commiserate and said she had no warning and wasn't told. She's a good soul and I don't hold anything against her. I don't hold anything against anyone. God always puts us where we're supposed to be and takes us out when it's time to move on.

Oh, when I left, I'm sure they changed the security keypad. When they'd give us a new code, they'd tell us what it stood for so we could remember it. The code when I left was D-I-C-E. Management told us it stood for "Do I Cut Expenses?" Great for morale.

I remember thinking it actually stood for "Do I Cut Employees?"

The Aftermath

That night I attended a dinner party with my boyfriend, Dean. I told him what had happened, but we kept our chins up and mouths shut. Kind of hard to eat that way.

The newspaper carried the story the next day and I eventually had to take my phone off the hook.

The first person to call me was Joan, who had left her network job to anchor the news at a large major market station. She asked me what my salary had been and I told her. Turns out that's what she was making in the major market.

The first person I called was my mother. I told her I had bad news and good news. She said give her the bad news first. I said, no, I had to give her the good news first – that I'd be able to be home for Christmas.

She was thrilled and asked why. I said, "That's the bad news." But, as usual, she was supportive and loving and I totally enjoyed my Christmas vacation.

Musical Stations

My agent tried sort of half-heartedly to get me another anchor job, but I'd had a good run and really didn't care. And I was 47, too old for a female news anchor back then.

Kent is 11 years older than I.

Sure enough, newspapers eventually ran the story that Kent had retired from WYFF when his contract expired.

I knew what that meant.

Before long he turned up anchoring the noon news on WSPA, where he worked for nine years, also anchoring at 5:30 P.M. Everyone I talked to inside and outside the business was happy he came out of "retirement" so soon. Way to go, Kent!

My Legacy

I had a lot of fans during my fifteen years of broadcasting and want all of them to know how much I still love and appreciate them.

I'd like to think I had a major impact on the area as the world's greatest newsman, er, newswoman. But that's not my legacy. I learned from former co-workers at both stations what my contribution to their news departments really was.

At WSPA, reporters and anchors wrote our stories on thick copy paper with electric typewriters, one copy of which ran through the teleprompter. I was hoping that I'd be able to write on a computer at WYFF but, alas, their typewriters were worse than WSPA's.

Not long after I left WSPA, I heard they'd gotten computers for the newsroom. But in my five years at WYFF we still used the same old electric typewriters.

After I left WYFF, a former co-worker told me they had a budget meeting with department heads asking for what they wanted and needed. The newsroom wanted computers but GM Dick said they couldn't afford them. Someone piped up, "Hey, Annette's gone; of course, we can afford them."

They got their computers.

Fellow broadcast journalists – you're welcome!

13
Life After Broadcasting

It wasn't time to retire so I had to figure out what I wanted to do now. I decided to work for myself coaching people in presentation and media skills.

I ran a weekly ad in the newspaper. My first client was a beauty contestant. We worked together once and her mother wrote me a check for $100.

My next client was the wife of our Lt. Governor who wanted help with her speaking skills.

I thought people would beat a path to my door since I was already known to be an expert in these areas. But I found out quickly it doesn't work that way.

One day I was walking through my apartment (I'd sold my house) and started feeling some panic setting in about how I was going to support myself. All of a sudden, I had a clear thought, which has kept me going ever since.

I thought, "*God got me this far. He won't drop me now.*"

Another? Unhappy Viewer

Remember in Chapter Two (page 10) I told you about the woman who called the newsroom complaining that I'd taken

Dan's job and should be out looking for a husband instead of anchoring the news?

I wondered if it was the same woman who called years later.

One day I came home to discover a dozen calls on my answering machine. The first eleven were hang-ups but the last one was a doozy. An angry woman's voice said, "Well, where are you – in bed with one of your *clients*? I know you're not doing speech coaching; you're in the prostitute house."

Click.

I remember telling my answering machine if that were true, I'd be making a lot more money. I hung up and then subscribed to the phone company's voice mail service.

Several months later on Thanksgiving Day, my phone rang. I answered. It was the same woman accusing me of being a prostitute and haranguing me for all sorts of sins. I tried reasoning with her but she had her say and hung up.

So, I dialed *69 and she answered. I asked her please not to hang up and she started screaming at me saying she was taking care of a sick husband and how dare I call and harass her. Poor lady couldn't have been in her right mind. As she hung up, I heard her say to someone, "Now they've got a way to call you back." I called again; she didn't answer but she gave her husband's name on her voice message. So, I looked up her address out of curiosity.

I talked to my brother about all this, wondering why she would call me and accuse me of such things. He said that when I was on TV she could yell at the screen and vent. But when I left, she couldn't do that so she called me in person.

Whatever the reason, she never called again. In the spirit of forgiveness, I sent her a Christmas card designed by a disabled person. She sent it back, criticizing me for sending her a card I got for free. O.K. We're done.

Back to business

I decided to add training as a service so I attended train-the-trainer workshops and joined two professional speakers' organizations. Before one workshop I received a questionnaire in the mail asking me to complete and mail back.

At the workshop one of the speakers gave us the results, which was our DISC behavioral style assessment. I'd never heard of that before and was blown away by how accurately it described me. I knew I had to use this assessment in my communications training. Other members told me about the company that created them — Target Training, Intl. I soon became a Value-Added Associate.

Eventually, I became a Certified Professional Behavioral and Values Analyst and use the assessments in my training, coaching, and consulting.

Meeting my Mentor

One of the steps I took when I first started my business was to talk with several executives and community leaders to get their advice on what I should do with my skills. One of them became my mentor. I'd met him and his wife during a WYFF fund-raiser.

WYFF carried the Childrens' Miracle Network Telethon each year. Once when I was one of the hosts, I sat down next to an older couple who was there to talk about their foster children.

The husband, Jim, was one of the most successful

businessmen in our area – or any area, for that matter. We chatted for a while and I was impressed with both of them.

I didn't call Jim often because I knew how busy he was as the Director of Food Services for Sara Lee. Once I called to get some advice; I was hesitating to take it and he chidingly said, "Annette, you should listen to your mentor." I would never have asked him to be my mentor and didn't think of him that way until he said that. How blessed I felt.

He was a big believer in using assessments for hiring and managing employees and executives. When he invited me to lunch one day, I had him fill out my questionnaire and boldly asked him what it would take for him to switch to using mine.

He said accuracy, speed of delivery, and cost. I gave him a free assessment and not only did he begin using my assessments with his company, he referred other business people to me.

At that meeting I asked him how I could best use the assessments to help businesses and he said, "Write down these three words: Find, Get, Keep.

"Companies want to find the best people, get the best people, and keep the best people."

So, I took his advice. I focused on helping companies improve employee selection and retention and am still doing it today.

I now facilitate a TTI process called Job Benchmarking that makes a virtual science out of selecting superior performers and retaining them.

An Unbelievable Tragedy

Jim continued to help me through the years and gave me a wonderful endorsement for my first book, *Why Can't You See it My Way? Resolving Values Conflicts at Work and Home.*

But one day watching the news, I heard a story that for me was worse than anything we'd ever reported when I was a news anchor.

Jim was missing. He was selling his SUV and had it parked across from a convenience store in an empty parking lot out in the country where he and his family lived.

His wife worried because he was supposed to attend a meeting that morning and one person he was meeting with called to find out why he didn't show up. He never missed or was even late for business meetings.

She drove to the spot where the SUV was parked and found his empty car there with the door open. The SUV was gone.

Police arrested a couple from Tennessee, who confessed and took them to a storage area where Jim's body was found in a freezer. They had put him in the back of the SUV and put duct tape on his mouth and nose. He suffocated and died.

Words can't describe how I felt and still feel about losing him. So, I won't try. I'll just say, "Thank you, Jim, for all the help you gave me and others you mentored. Thank you for being one of the best, most unselfish people I've ever known. God bless you."

14

Film at 11:00

During my early days in television, I always thought if I wrote a book about it I'd entitle it, "Film at 11:00." But Maggie Bloom has already taken that title, so I hope she doesn't mind if I use it as my final chapter heading.

Read the Preface to this book for one of the funniest stories and see that I had another title in mind, but I used it instead as the heading for Chapter 9.

Here's how that almost-title came about – perhaps the funniest rumor about me, based on a true event.

One day after I'd been out of TV news for a while, Dean and I were having lunch in a small café. A woman came up to me and asked, "Are you Annette Estes?"

"Yes."

She queried, "May I ask you a question?" I said, "Sure."

She asked, "Did you really say, 'It's too hot to F***' on TV?"

I don't know what possessed me, but not missing a beat I looked her in the eye and said, "Honey, it's *never* too hot to F***!"

Her eyes became saucers and she walked away. Dean and I had a good laugh.

So, when Scott (see the Preface) called me that day I knew what he meant when he told me he and his buddies always thought of me when it was extremely hot. I want to thank both of them for giving me the impetus to write this book. It's been fun and I hope you've enjoyed reading it as much as I have writing it.

As I said before, life has taught me that something good always comes from a bad situation. After beginning my own business, I was hired by a group to do a media skills workshop. The next morning, I was giving a summary to the participants and advised them to be very careful of what they said if they were anywhere near a microphone.

They all laughed, applauded, and gave me a standing ovation. The elephant in the room lumbered out.

During my fifteen years as a news anchor, I was privileged to speak to many civic clubs and other groups. Once when the club president introduced me, I stood, paused, and looked at everyone. I said, "You all look so much younger and thinner in person." Lots of laughter, but no standing ovation.

I just thought of another funny story about something that happened at WSPA-TV.

Our program director was a very proper and soft-spoken gentleman. One day he was in the newsroom and told some of us about a call he'd gotten from an irate viewer who had called him a "f***ing a**hole."

He looked at us and said (in his stateliest voice) that he told the caller, "I am *not* a f***ing a**hole."

Looking back on my career, I'd do some things differently and some the same. Since learning how to better understand people's behaviors and motivators, I've thought if I knew then what I know now, I could own one of those stations. No matter what business you're in, or for and with whom you work, people skills are your most valuable asset.

One thing I would do differently is based on the first sentence of Chapter 1 and that old saying, "Be careful what you want; you'll probably get it."

At some point during my career, I decided I wanted to be successful enough to earn a six-figure income. The universe answered and I got it in my final year as a news anchor.

Many times over the years since, I've thought, "*Why didn't I say a seven-figure income?*" I'd probably still be anchoring. Nah.

Happily, WYFF will be paying me until I die. In just three more years my pension check earnings will surpass $86,000.

I can live with that.

Two Somethings Good from Bad

This story is about a Georgia state trooper who, with help from a reporter, probably saved my career. When I was in Atlanta covering the Democratic National Convention, WYFF wanted me to interview our state's governor during their noon newscast.

All of us media folk were stationed in the basement of an Omni annex building. I climbed the stairs and as I walked outside, I realized I'd forgotten to hang my credentials around my neck and knew I wouldn't be able to get into the Omni.

I panicked and the trooper standing near the door asked what was wrong. I told him and he came to the rescue. He got on his walkie-talkie, called down to our news team, and asked someone to bring my credentials up pronto.

Our reporter, Randy, ran upstairs and gave them to me. I made it with seconds to spare. (Randy had gone on the Germany trip with us. He was one of the good guys.)

The next day when I walked out to go over to the Omni, *with* my credentials, the trooper was there. He smiled and gave me a button that read, "Don't Panic!" He also gave me a coffee mug with the Georgia State Patrol logo on it.

I have the button still on my office bulletin board and I still drink coffee out of the mug.

And the best part, David and his wife Barbara exchange Christmas cards with me every year.

Now, my final story. I'd been out of TV for more than twenty years and had moved to Iowa. My two favorite radio personalities were still doing their morning show back from where I'd moved. One day I got a phone call from one of them wanting to do a "Whatever Happened to..." telephone interview with me.

Of course, they wanted to focus on the Black Wednesday event. He said they wanted me to say on their radio show what I'd said that day that made me infamous. I said, "Are you kidding me? No way." He said I had to, it would be so funny. And he promised they'd bleep it out.

So, I decided to be a good sport and said it again. "Why don't they check the f***ing mics??!!" Thanks, guys. It was fun. And cathartic.

Lessons Learned

Vernon Law said, "Experience is a hard teacher because she gives the test first, the lesson afterward." How true that is.

So, what advice can I give you from lessons I learned as a television news anchor?

- Some people love us; some hate us. You can't please everyone.
- If someone doesn't like you, it's their problem not yours.
- If you love your job and it comes easy to you, sometimes make it look like you're struggling so your boss and co-workers will think you're working hard.
- Again, something good always comes from a bad situation. Sometimes something great!
- Nothing is permanent; change is good.
- If you meet celebrities don't gush over them; treat them like they're normal people, because they are.
- Do your job to the best of your ability and go the extra mile.
- Know that your boss doesn't want complaints. She wants solutions.
- If your boss piles more work on you than you can get done in time, then adds another task, ask him which of the other jobs you can drop in order to get it all done.
- Don't let people bully or intimidate you.
- Be honest; admit your mistakes; apologize.
- Learn from your mistakes.
- Be kind to your co-workers. One of them might write a book someday and tell the world that you're not. (Of course, the author may not reveal your real name but you, and others, will know who you are.)
- Understand people's behavioral styles and practice the Platinum Rule: "Treat others the way *they* want to be treated."

- Have a positive attitude. Always.
- Realize what Richard Carlson wrote is true: "Don't Sweat the Small Stuff ... and it's all small stuff."
- Take comfort in knowing what CoachU founder Thomas Leonard said is true: "We're all doing the best we can, even when we know we're not."
- Don't say the "F" word on TV. Then again....

And finally, when you're worried about the future, know with certainty that:

God got you this far.
He won't drop you now.

Photo Gallery

Photo Gallery

Annette with CBS News anchor
Walter Cronkite

Annette with NBC News anchor
Tom Brokaw

Annette with CBS News anchor
Dan Rather

Annette with *60 Minutes* anchor
Mike Wallace

Annette's WLKY-TV colleague
Diane Sawyer

Annette interviewed Peter Jennings
at WLKY-TV

TV listing for half-hour special, 1980

Photo Gallery

Annette interviews VP candidate George H. W. Bush in 1980

The candidates support Annette at the
1980 Democratic National Convention

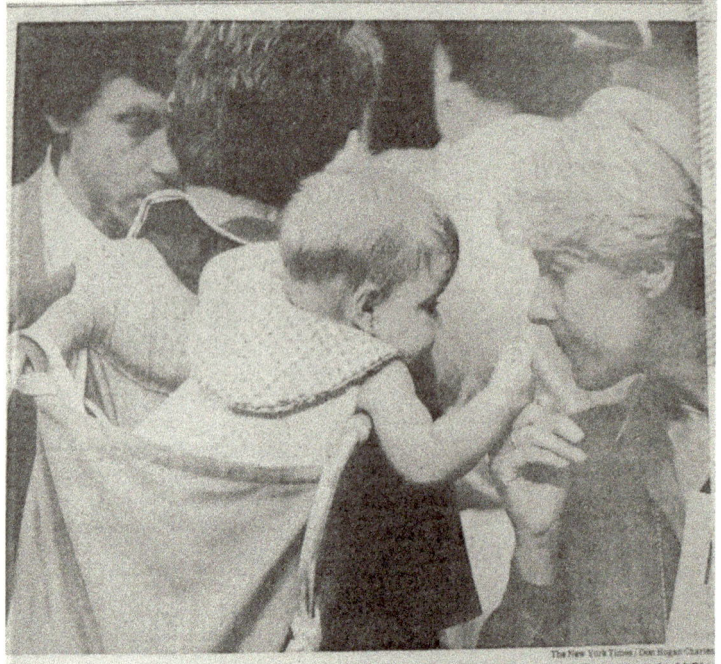

Annette meets Giovanna at the 1980
Democratic National Convention in NYC
New York Times, Page B1

The photographer who took this picture was Don Hogan Charles, the first black photographer hired by the *Times*, who was renowned for his photos taken during the civil rights era. He died in 2017.

EMAIL FROM GIOVANNA
May, 2019

Hi Annette. I can't tell you how wonderful it was to find your note on my desk yesterday at the end of a busy day and to be able to share it with my father. So neat to reconnect with you in this way -- Google really is something! I do have a very yellowed copy of the photo and, for many years, my father has told me stories about this day and the convention in 1980.

Thanks so much for taking the time to track me down -- a very special surprise.

By the way, I love the title of your book and look forward to reading it!

Take care,
Gia

FROM HER PARENTS

Dear Annette,

Thank you for your persistence in tracking Giovanna down. That picture is in our Hall of Fame moments, for sure. Walter Cronkite stopped by to give Gia a little 'chin tickle' that day, a memory I'm sure he treasures.

I attended 3 DNConventions, the first in 1964 after the Kennedy assassination, 1980, and the last one in 1996. Each one different, all interesting.

You had a very interesting and full career, each day new stories and meeting new people in your extended community. It must have been a most stimulating career.

I hope you enjoy your new life.

With gratitude,

Jim and Clorinda Leddy

Mouthing Off

Annette with
Anthony Hopkins

Annette chats with
James Earl Jones

Annette with
Tom Selleck

Annette interviews
Tom Selleck

Annette with
Larry Hagman

Annette with
Ken Howard

Photo Gallery

George C. Scott as Gen. George S. Patton
Annette's first celebrity interview

Bonnie Franklin, who shared
Annette's birthday

Annette with
Valerie Bertinelli

Annette interviews Dukes of Hazzard cast Tom Wopat,
Catherine Bach, and John Schneider

Mouthing Off

Annette with
Patrick Duffy

Annette interviews
Vic Tayback

Annette interviews
Linda Gray

Annette interviews
Ed Asner

Annette interviews
Buddy Ebsen

Annette chats with
Celia Weston

www.ingramcontent.com/pod-product-compliance
Lightning Source LLC
Chambersburg PA
CBHW021017090426
42738CB00007B/809